Penny's Pock

A tale of a sibling brought home through a gestational carrier

ISBN:0-692-84772-3
ISBN-13:978-0-692-84772-5

DEDICATION

Dedicated to Danielle, Neil, Abigail, and Aiden G.

ACKNOWLEDGMENTS

My husband and I would like to acknowledge the clinicians and nurses at the Center for Reproductive Medicine who help families dream the impossible and make it happen.

The O'Possum family was like a lot of happy families you may know. Mama, Papa, and Polly O'Possum liked to spend summer days playing together outside at the park.

Polly also liked to play dress up and Papa played along. Polly thought her daddy looked beautiful as a princess. Papa thought... well, he loved playing with Polly no matter how he looked.

When Mama and Papa were busy with work, Polly played with her toys. She was usually happy drawing, playing picnic, or doing puzzles. But sometimes, Polly wanted to play jump rope or board games. It was hard to play these by herself. Polly knew it was be easier if she had a brother or sister.

Polly always felt loved;

but sometimes, she felt lonely, too.

Polly asked her mom why some friends have brothers and sisters and she didn't. Mama O'Possum explained that families come in all sizes. Mama hugged Polly tight and told her she was very special. Then, she showed Polly her pocket, where baby opossums grow until they are big enough to come out on their own. Mama's pocket had gotten a hole in it and could no longer hold a tiny baby safely.

Polly understood her mommy couldn't carry more babies. But that didn't stop her from wanting one. Her parents still wanted Polly to have a brother or sister, too. There did not seem be a way, until a kind friend named Ms. Penny gave them a generous idea.

She loved the O'Possum family. So, she asked if she could share her healthy pocket with Mama.   She could carry Mama and Papa O'Possum's new baby in it!

And do you know what the family said?

The O'Possum family said, "Yes!"

Mama and Papa then met the doctor who put a tiny baby, who was part Mama and part Papa, into Ms. Penny's pocket. The baby was so small that the doctor needed a microscope to see it.

Ms. Penny promised to give it a safe place to grow until it was big and strong enough to go home with the O'Possum family.

For Polly, it seemed like **forever** for the baby to grow big enough. But her mommy explained that all families wait a while before their new brother or sister is born and can come home. She reminded Polly that there was a lot to do to get ready for a new baby.   Mama O'Possum sorted baby clothes, Papa put the crib back together, and Polly made welcome home signs.

The most fun part of getting ready for a new baby was picking out a name. Mama, Papa, and Polly each wrote down their favorites.

What name did they choose?

Finally, the exciting day came! The tiny baby wasn't tiny anymore. She was big enough to leave Ms. Penny's pocket and come home. Polly stayed with Grandma and Grandpa while Mama and Papa drove quickly to the hospital.

When Ms. Penny placed the new baby, Piper O'Possum into Mama's arms, Ms. Penny felt like she had just given the O'Possum family the best gift ever. But little Piper's biggest gift was yet to come....

...a lifetime of love given to baby Piper by

her **new big sister!**

ABOUT THE AUTHOR

Elizabeth Hebl is a family physician and mom with an infertility journey. She searched for a way to explain her infertility to her young daughter. Her daughter once asked if her tummy was broken and couldn't hold any more babies. That was the start of Dr. Hebl's quest to draw and write about a fictional animal family in a way that helped children understand the love and dedication needed to pursue non traditional family building. Dr. Hebl's goal is to remind children conceived through assisted reproductive technology that their story starts not with science, but with love.

Made in the USA
Middletown, DE
31 October 2024

63656066R00018